SAVE THE
POLAR BEAR

Sarah Eason

PowerKiDS press

New York

Published in 2009 by The Rosen Publishing Group, Inc.
29 East 21st Street, New York, NY 10010

Illustrators: Andrew Geeson and Marijke Van Veldhoven
Designer: Paul Myerscough
Consultant: Michael Scott
U.S. Editor: Kara Murray

Photo Credits: Ardea/M. Watson front cover; Corbis/Wolfgang Kaehler p.26 /Galen Rowell p.29; Digital Vision/Joel Simon p.4, p.6, p.7, p.9, p.10, p.18, p.20, p.24, p.28, poster; Dreamstime p.15, p.23; FLPA/Flip Nicklin/Minden Pictures p.27 /Konrad Wothe/Minden Pictures p.17; istockphoto p.8, p.11, p.16, p.22, p.25; Photos.com p.12, p.14, p.21; Shutterstock p.5, p.13, p.19.

Library of Congress Cataloging-in-Publication Data

Eason, Sarah.
  Save the polar bear / Sarah Eason. — 1st ed.
      p. cm. — (Save the)
  Includes index.
  ISBN 978-1-4358-2810-0 (library binding)
  1. Polar bear—Juvenile literature. I. Title.
  QL737.C27E17 2009
  599.786—dc22

                          2008027039

Printed in China

Contents

Why Are Polar Bears So Special?

Polar bears are the biggest land-living meat eaters on Earth. Male polar bears can grow up to 8 feet (2.5 m) long – that's much taller than an average man. Polar bears weigh as much as 1,433 pounds (650 kg).

SAVE THE POLAR BEAR!

There are many things that you can do to help save the polar bear. Look out for the Save the Polar Bear boxes in this book for ways in which you and your friends can help.

Polar bears are one of the few animals that can survive in the freezing **Arctic**. They are great swimmers and can swim many miles from **ice pack** to ice pack in search of the seals that they eat.

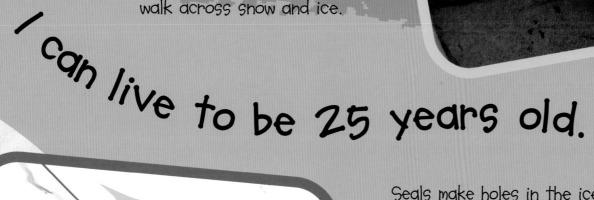

My large, flat feet are like giant snowshoes. They help me walk across snow and ice.

I can live to be 25 years old.

Seals make holes in the ice. They use them to dive into the water to hunt for fish and come up again for air. I lie by ice holes and wait for seals to surface.

Did You Know?

My fur helps gather the heating rays of the Sun to keep me warm.

Why Is the Polar Bear in Danger?

I can survive without food for a fe

You have probably heard of global warming. You may have heard that this is harming our planet by changing its climate. But did you know that it is also threatening the polar bear?

Did You Know?

There are about 25,000 polar bears in the world today. We could be gone forever in just 90 years if more is not done to protect our habitat.

Global warming has made the Arctic summers longer. More Arctic ice melts during the summer, which forces the polar bear onto land. Polar bears eat seals, which live on ice. When the ice disappears, the polar bear can no longer hunt and must go without food.

Seals have a thick layer of fat, called **blubber**. Blubber has a lot of energy for me – I eat it to help me survive in the cold.

...onths, but if Arctic summers become longer, I will starve.

SAVE THE POLAR BEAR!

Switch off your lights, TV and radio when you do not need them. You will help **stop** climate change and help save the polar bear.

Until my brother and I are old enough to hunt for ourselves, our mother must hunt for us.

Where Do Polar Bears Live?

Polar bears live in a place called the Arctic. This is a very cold area near the North Pole. Most of the Arctic is not land, but sea. For much of the year, the sea is frozen into a huge area of sea ice. Polar bears wander far out onto the sea ice to hunt for seals.

I live on

SAVE THE POLAR BEAR!

Driving to the supermarket adds to global warming. Try to do your shopping in local shops or ask your parents if you can visit your local farmers' market.

Polar bears swim slowly and steadily by paddling with their front paws. They can swim without stopping for a few days. Their thick layer of body fat helps them float in the sea.

I spend most of my time **roaming** across ice packs, hunting for seals to eat.

land near the sea during summer.

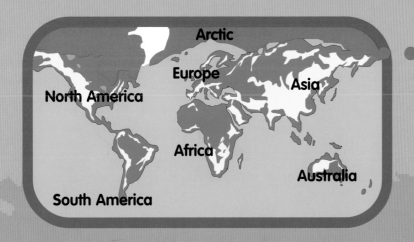

The red area on this map is the Arctic. Polar bears live close to the sea all over the Arctic.

Did You Know?

I can swim more than 40 miles (65 km)!

What Do Polar Bears Look Like?

Polar bears have thick fur and a thick layer of fat. This keeps them warm in the freezing Arctic weather. In fact, because their furry coat keeps them so warm, they must move slowly so they do not get too hot!

My waterproof fur keeps me warm in icy

small ears

thick white fur

strong legs

sharp claws and furry feet

I am a male polar bear. I grow much taller than female bears. I am nearly 8 feet (2.5 m) tall and weigh as much as six people.

I get very hot on sunny days. To cool down, I **pant**, like a dog, and stretch out in the cold snow.

Arctic water.

Did You Know?

The largest-ever polar bear measured 11 feet (3.5 m) from nose to tail.

How Do Polar Bears Make a Home?

Adult polar bears live alone. Each polar bear has its own territory where it lives and hunts. A polar bear's territory must be very large so that it can find enough seals to eat.

Sometimes I walk

sniff, sniff

Polar bears wander far out onto the huge ice pack, searching for food. They curl up on the ice to sleep. Polar bear territories are so big that bears do not often meet each other.

I save energy by napping during the day. If I save energy, I will need to catch fewer seals.

for days to look for food.

I sometimes dig a small hole in the snow. I hide inside the hole during stormy weather.

Did You Know?

A polar bear's territory can be as big as 80,000 square miles (200,000 sq km)!

What Do Polar Bears Eat?

Polar bears hunt alone. They mainly eat seals, but sometimes eat walrus, whales, squid, fish and seaweed. If polar bears find a big meal, such as a dead whale, they may share it with other bears.

SAVE THE POLAR BEAR!

When polar bears eat fish and seals that have swallowed polluted water, they become ill. Write a letter to your congressman to ask what they are doing to stop pollution of the sea.

Seals give birth to their pups in holes beneath snow on top of the sea ice. The holes are called lairs. Polar bears break into the lairs and eat the **seal pups** inside.

This seal has come up for air. I can dive underwater and hold my breath for two minutes. That helps me creep up on seals on top of the ice.

My sharp claws help me grab my prey.

Did You Know?

Polar bears can smell a seal under the ice from .5 mile (1 km) away!

My white fur helps me hide in the snow so I can creep up on seals.

Can Polar Bears Survive Without Food?

In summer, the Arctic ice begins to melt and it is difficult for polar bears to hunt for seals. Polar bears must then look for food on land. They can survive on very little food in the summer because they get energy from the fat they stored in the winter.

SAVE THE POLAR BEAR!

You can help stop climate change by biking or walking to school instead of driving.

16

There is very little food for polar bears to eat on land, and some bears will wander 124 miles (200 km) inland to find food. Hungry polar bears dig up plant roots and eat grass and berries. Some lucky bears even manage to catch and eat birds.

If I am really hungry, I eat trash left by people. Trash can give me a stomachache and make me ill, so it is not my favorite food.

I sometimes eat bird eggs if I find them on the beach.

I love eating seaweed. It tastes delicious! I look for seaweed on the beach. Sometimes I dive to the bottom of the sea to find it.

How Do Polar Bears Talk?

Polar bears show each other how they feel by making lots of different grunting and growling sounds. When they are angry or frightened, they hiss and roar.

I charge at other

SAVE THE POLAR BEAR!

Ask your parents if you can turn down the heat in your house. This will help stop global warming.

grunt, grunt

18

When I shake, growl and show my teeth, it tells other bears that I am strong and ready to fight.

bears to scare them away.

To make friends, polar bears walk around each other in a circle and make quiet grunting sounds. Then they touch noses to say hello. Sometimes they will wrestle to find out who is the strongest!

We are young polar bears. We like to play fight in the snow.

How Do Polar Bears Find a Mate?

Polar bears **mate** in the spring, from April to June. When they reach six years old, female polar bears can begin to have **cubs**. Males begin to mate at about three years old.

I eat lots

Did You Know?

After mating, the male leaves. The female polar bear raises her cubs by herself.

I am fighting another male polar bear because we both want to mate with the same female. If I win the fight, I can mate with the female and she will have my cubs.

of food before my cubs are born.

Fluffing out my fur makes me look bigger and stronger. I growl and swagger to scare other males away from my female.

A male polar bear sniffs the air to find the **scent** of a female polar bear. He can smell her from far away and follows her scent until he finds her.

How Do Polar Bears Care for Their Babies?

When I was

In November, the female polar bear digs a hole, called a **den**, in the snow. She will give birth to her babies there. Baby polar bears are called cubs. Mother polar bears usually give birth to two cubs.

Did You Know?

Mother polar bears can go without food for five months while they care for their cubs in the den.

When my brother and I were born, we were only 12 inches (30 cm) long – that's as small as a rat. We couldn't hear until we were four weeks old and didn't open our eyes until we were nearly five weeks old.

A mother polar bear stays in the den for four to five months before she gives birth to her cubs. She cuddles her cubs to keep them warm. Newborn cubs do not have teeth, so they drink milk from their mother's teats.

I keep my cubs safe and warm in my den until they are big enough to go outside.

born, I weighed less than a bag of sugar!

How Do Young Polar Bears Grow Up?

By March, the mother polar bear has used up nearly all of her body fat and is beginning to feel very hungry. The family now need to leave the safety of the den and go in search of food.

When we are

SAVE THE POLAR BEAR!

Airplanes are one cause of global warming. You can help stop global warming by going on a vacation close to home instead of flying.

24

The hungry family set out on the long walk to the coast to find seals to eat. The mother polar bear catches seals for her cubs until they learn how to hunt on their own. The cubs learn how to hunt by watching their mother.

I am sniffing the air for danger. I must keep my cubs away from male polar bears until they are big enough to take care of themselves.

three years old, we will hunt on our own.

My brother and I have just left our den for the first time. We are play fighting in the snow.

Did You Know?

A mother polar bear must catch at least two seals a week to feed her family.

Can Polar Bears and People Live Together?

Polar bears were once so hunted by humans that they nearly became **extinct**. It is now **illegal** to hunt polar bears. Only **native people**, whose ancestors have lived in the Arctic for thousands of years, are allowed to hunt a few bears.

People used to

The Inuit people have lived in the Arctic for thousands of years. Inuits are allowed to hunt some polar bears each year. They make their clothes from polar bear skin.

polar bear skin

Big companies drill for oil in the Arctic sea. Leaks from oil tankers can pollute the sea.

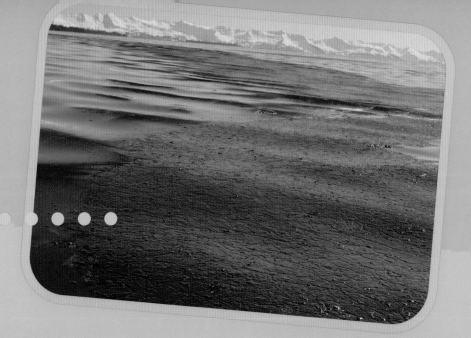

Poisonous chemicals from land are carried to the Arctic on the wind and in the sea. Pollution can make us very ill.

hunt us for our skins or for fun.

When we are hungry, we sometimes look for food near towns. This can make people very frightened, and they may shoot us if we come too close.

Did You Know?

In 1950 only 5,000 polar bears existed.

What Can You Do to Help Polar Bears?

Many people in the world are trying to help polar bears. There are lots of ways in which you can help, too.

Did You Know?

Although it is against the law to hunt us, many polar bears are still illegally killed for our fur.

Find out more about how you can help save polar bears and their habitat by visiting this Web site:

www.powerkidslinks.com/savethe/pbear/

Why not adopt a polar bear?

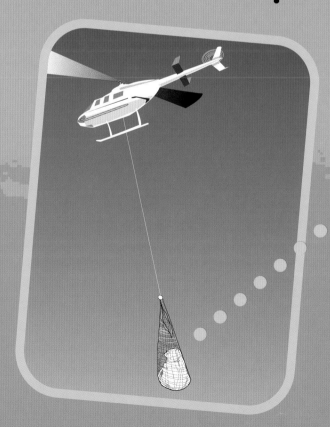

These **scientists** are taking a small amount of blood from me. They can test the blood to find out how much pollution I have in my body.

Sometimes we wander too far from our territories in search of food. When this happens, we may be captured and kept safe until winter returns in the Arctic. Then we are airlifted by helicopter back to our natural habitat, where we can hunt again for food.

Glossary

Arctic (ARK-tik) The area of frozen sea and land around the North Pole.

blubber (BLUH-ber) The thick layer of fat under an animal's skin.

charge (CHAHRJ) When an animal runs very fast towards another animal.

climate change (KLY-mit CHAYNJ) A big change in the weather over a long time, now made worse by human pollution.

cub (KUB) A baby polar bear.

den (DEN) A home or hiding place of a wild animal.

extinct (ek-STINKT) When an animal or plant has died out forever.

global warming (GLOH-bul WARM-ing) A change in the climate that makes the world warm up. Global warming is caused by pollution made by humans.

habitat (HA-beh-tat) Where an animal or plant naturally lives.

ice pack (YS PAK) Solid ice covering the sea.

illegal (ih-LEE-gul) Against the law.

mate (MAYT) When male and female animals make babies.

native people (NAY-tiv PEE-pul) People who belong to a group that has lived in the same place for thousands of years.

pant (PANT) When animals breathe quickly through their mouths to cool down.

poisonous chemicals (POYZ-nus KEH-mih-kulz) Chemicals that harm animals and the environment.

pollute (puh-LOOT) To spoil with harmful chemicals or gases.

pollution (puh-LOO-shun) Harmful chemicals or gases that spoil the environment.

roam (ROHM) To wander around.

scent (SENT) The smell of an animal or plant.

scientists (SY-un-tists) People who make a careful study of the world around them.

seal pups (SEEL PUPS) Baby seals.

Index